Emotional Independence: Self-Reliance

By Jermaine Alexander

Acknowledgments

To Granny,

Your love has been the quiet, steady foundation beneath every word of this book. More than just a cherished family member, you have been an unwavering source of inspiration, a fountain of wisdom, and the most constant believer in my dreams. Your stories, your laughter, and the gentle strength you've always embodied have shaped me in profound ways, teaching me the true meaning of resilience and the power of an anchored spirit.

Thank you for the countless lessons, the endless encouragement, and for simply being you. This book, and the journey it represents, would not have been possible without your light guiding my path.

With all my love and deepest gratitude,

Mann

Introduction:

Reclaiming Your Inner Anchor

In a world that constantly pulls us outward, demanding our attention, dictating our worth, and often subtly suggesting that our happiness lies in external validation—it's easy to feel adrift. We chase approval, cling to relationships out of fear of loneliness, and allow the opinions of others to dictate our inner peace. This pervasive pattern, often subtle yet profoundly impactful, is what we call **emotional dependence**. It's the quiet concession of our true self, a persistent belief that our emotional well-being is contingent upon someone or something outside of us.

Perhaps you recognize this feeling: the subtle anxiety when a text isn't immediately returned, the tendency to self-abandon in favor of pleasing others, the constant seeking of reassurance, or the gnawing feeling that you're not quite whole without a partner, a certain job, or external accolades. You are not alone. In an age of unprecedented connectivity, genuine self-reliance can feel like a forgotten art.

But what if your happiness wasn't a fragile gift bestowed by others, but an inherent wellspring within you? What if your sense of worth wasn't a fluctuating stock market, but an unshakeable inner knowing?

This book is an invitation to embark on a transformative journey toward **emotional independence**. It is not a call to isolation, nor does it advocate for emotional detachment. On the contrary, true emotional independence is the bedrock upon which the most profound, authentic, and fulfilling connections are built. When you are whole within yourself, you enter relationships from a place of abundance and choice, not desperate need. You give and receive love more freely, capable of navigating life's inevitable challenges with grace, and standing firm in your own truth.

Over the coming chapters, we will explore the subtle ways emotional dependence takes root, often stemming from early experiences and societal conditioning. We will then systematically dismantle the reliance on external anchors, guiding you through the essential pillars of:

- **Self-Awareness:** Understanding your unique emotional landscape, values, and needs.
- **Self-Validation:** Becoming your own most trusted source of worth and reassurance.
- **Self-Responsibility:** Reclaiming your agency and owning your responses to life.
- **Healthy Boundaries:** Protecting your energy and defining your sacred space.

Beyond these foundations, you will discover how to cultivate a powerful inner strength—learning to manage your emotions, build unshakeable self-trust and confidence, embrace the enriching power of solitude, and cultivate resilience in the face of adversity. Finally, we will explore how this newfound independence transforms your relationships, allowing for true interdependence, and ignites your deepest purpose and passions.

This journey requires courage, curiosity, and a willingness to look inward. It is a path of profound self-discovery, leading you not just to freedom *from* dependence, but to the boundless freedom *of* being truly, unconditionally, and unapologetically you. The time to reclaim your inner anchor is now. Let's begin.

Part 1: Understanding Emotional Dependence

Chapter 1: What is Emotional Independence (and Dependence)?

To truly understand and cultivate emotional independence, we must first clearly define what it means – and, perhaps more importantly, what it *doesn't* mean. Often, the term is misunderstood, conjuring images of stoicism, aloofness, or a solitary existence. This couldn't be further from the truth. Emotional independence is not about being cold, detached, or uncaring; it's about being profoundly connected to yourself, allowing for richer, more authentic connections with others.

Let's start by clarifying the spectrum, from emotional dependence to true emotional independence.

Defining Emotional Dependence: The External Anchor

At its core, **emotional dependence** is a state where an individual's emotional well-being, self-worth, and happiness are primarily anchored in external sources. This means that your feelings, decisions, and sense of identity are heavily influenced, or even dictated, by the actions, opinions, approval, or presence of others.

Think of it like a boat that constantly needs to be tethered to a dock to feel secure. Without that external connection, it feels lost, adrift, or unstable.

Key characteristics of emotional dependence often include:

- **Reliance on external validation:** Your self-worth fluctuates based on how others perceive you, their compliments, or their approval. You constantly seek reassurance.
- **Fear of abandonment:** An intense anxiety about being left alone, leading to people-pleasing behaviors, avoiding conflict, or tolerating unhealthy dynamics to keep someone close.
- **Difficulty making decisions independently:** You might constantly seek advice or approval from others before making choices, fearing making the "wrong" one or being judged.
- **Emotional reactivity:** Your mood and emotional state are highly susceptible to the actions or moods of others. If someone is upset, you become upset. If they are happy, you are happy.
- **Taking things personally:** Assuming responsibility for others' feelings or reactions, even when they have nothing to do with you.
- **Lack of clear boundaries:** Struggling to say "no," allowing others to overstep, or feeling guilty when asserting your needs.
- **Blurred sense of self:** Your identity might be deeply intertwined with a relationship or a role, making it hard to know who you are without that external connection.
- **Emotional "emptiness" when alone:** A pervasive feeling of loneliness, anxiety, or boredom when not actively engaged with others.

It's important to note that a certain degree of "interdependence" is healthy in relationships. We are social beings, and our emotions are influenced by our interactions. The problem arises when this influence becomes a *necessity* for your well-being, where your inner state is largely *controlled* by external factors.

Defining Emotional Independence: The Inner Anchor

Now, let's turn to **emotional independence**. This is a state where an individual's emotional well-being, self-worth, and happiness are primarily anchored **within themselves**. It means having the inner resources to navigate your emotions, validate your experiences, and make choices that align with your authentic self, regardless of external circumstances.

To return to our analogy, an emotionally independent person is like a sturdy boat with its own strong anchor. It can connect to a dock (healthy relationships) and enjoy the stability, but it can also drop its own anchor and feel secure and stable in open water, able to withstand storms, and confident in its own course.

Key characteristics of emotional independence include:

- **Self-validation:** Your self-worth comes from within. You value your own opinions, feelings, and experiences, and don't constantly need external praise or approval to feel good about yourself.
- **Comfort with solitude:** You are comfortable being alone and can find peace, contentment, and even joy in your own company.
- **Clear and healthy boundaries:** You can assert your needs, say "no" when necessary, and protect your emotional and energetic space without guilt.
- **Emotional regulation:** You have developed strategies to manage your emotions effectively. You feel your feelings, but you don't allow them to overwhelm or dictate your actions.
- **Internal locus of control:** You recognize that while you cannot control external events or other people's actions, you *can* control your own reactions, choices, and attitude.
- **Authenticity:** You are true to yourself, expressing your genuine thoughts and feelings, rather than trying to be who you think others want you to be.
- **Resilience:** You have the capacity to bounce back from setbacks, disappointments, and challenges, drawing on your inner strength.
- **Growth mindset:** You view challenges as opportunities for learning and personal development, rather than threats to your emotional stability.

The Spectrum: From Dependence to Independence

It's crucial to understand that emotional independence isn't an "on/off" switch. It's a spectrum, and most people fall somewhere in the middle, exhibiting traits of both dependence and independence in different areas or relationships.

- **Highly Dependent:** Constantly seeking approval, unable to be alone, dramatic emotional shifts based on others' moods.

- **Moderately Dependent:** Can function independently but struggles with decision-making without input, fears conflict, or is highly sensitive to criticism.
- **Interdependent (Healthy):** Values connection and support from others, but can function autonomously. Self-worth is internal, not external. Gives and receives support freely.
- **Emotionally Independent:** Primarily self-validated, comfortable with solitude, possesses strong boundaries, can regulate emotions, and chooses connections from a place of wholeness.

My goal in this book is not to push you to the extreme of never needing anyone. That's neither healthy nor realistic. Humans are wired for connection. Instead, the aim is to empower you to move along the spectrum *towards* emotional independence, so that your connections are a **choice** born of genuine desire and shared strength, rather than a **need** driven by fear or a perceived lack within yourself.

In the following chapters, we will explore the deep roots of emotional dependence, understand its true costs, and then systematically build the pillars of inner strength that will allow you to cultivate profound emotional independence and live a life of authenticity and freedom.

Chapter 2: The Roots of Dependence: Where Does It Come From?

Understanding what emotional dependence is, and isn't, is the first step. The next crucial step is to explore its origins. Emotional dependence doesn't typically appear overnight; it's often a deeply ingrained pattern, shaped by a complex interplay of early life experiences, societal messages, cultural influences, and even individual temperament. Uncovering these roots isn't about assigning blame, but about gaining crucial **self-awareness**. When you understand *why* you might lean on external anchors, you're better equipped to consciously build your internal ones.

Let's explore some of the most common wellsprings of emotional dependence.

Childhood Experiences: The Blueprint of Attachment

Our earliest relationships, particularly with primary caregivers, lay down the fundamental blueprints for how we relate to ourselves and others. The quality of these early bonds significantly influences our adult attachment styles and our propensity for emotional dependence.

- **Inconsistent or Unresponsive Caregiving:** If a child's emotional needs were met inconsistently, or if their expressions of emotion were dismissed, punished, or ignored, they might learn that their feelings aren't valid or that they must earn love and attention. This can lead to a pervasive sense of insecurity and a constant need for external validation.
  - *Example:* A child who only receives comfort when they are sick might subconsciously learn to create drama or distress to get attention, carrying this pattern into adult relationships.
- **Overprotective or Enmeshed Parenting:** In some cases, parents, out of love, might overly control a child's experiences, make all their decisions, or discourage independent thought and action. This can prevent a child from developing their own sense of self-efficacy and problem-solving skills, leading to a feeling of helplessness without external direction. Enmeshment (where boundaries between parent and child are blurred) can make it difficult for an adult to form an identity separate from their family of origin.
- **Conditional Love:** If a child felt loved only when they met certain expectations, achieved specific accomplishments, or behaved in a particular way, they may internalize the belief that their worth is conditional. As adults, they might constantly strive for perfection or people-please to secure affection and approval.
- **Trauma or Abandonment:** Experiences of neglect, emotional or physical abuse, or actual abandonment in childhood can create deep-seated fears. These individuals might develop hyper-vigilance in relationships, an intense fear of being alone, or a desperate need to cling to others, even in unhealthy relationships, to avoid re-experiencing the pain of abandonment.

These early experiences aren't destiny, but they form powerful unconscious patterns. Recognizing how your early environment shaped your emotional landscape is a critical step towards rewiring those patterns.

Societal and Cultural Influences: The Messages We Absorb

Beyond our families, the broader societal and cultural narratives we absorb can also subtly (or overtly) promote emotional dependence.

- **Romanticized Codependence:** Popular culture, particularly in movies and songs, often glorifies intense, all-consuming romantic love where two people "complete" each other. While beautiful in fiction, this often promotes an unhealthy ideal of merging identities and relying solely on a partner for happiness, rather than cultivating individual wholeness.
- **Conformity and Approval:** Many societies value conformity and adherence to group norms. From a young age, we're often implicitly taught that fitting in and gaining approval from peers, teachers, or authority figures is crucial for acceptance and success. This can translate into an adult who prioritizes external approval over their own inner voice.
- **Gender Roles:** Traditional gender roles can sometimes reinforce dependence. For instance, historical expectations for women to be emotionally supportive, nurturing, and reliant on men, or for men to be stoic providers who suppress their emotions, can create imbalances and hinder emotional autonomy.
- **Social Media and External Validation:** In the digital age, social media platforms have amplified the drive for external validation. Likes, comments, and follower counts can become addictive forms of external approval, constantly encouraging us to curate an image that pleases others rather than reflecting our authentic selves.

Fear of Abandonment and Loneliness: The Primal Drivers

At a fundamental level, much emotional dependence stems from a primal fear: the fear of being alone, unloved, or rejected. This fear can manifest as:

- **People-Pleasing:** A pervasive need to accommodate others' wishes, avoid conflict, and never upset anyone, even at the expense of your own needs and boundaries. The underlying belief is often, "If I'm not perfect or if I displease them, they will leave me."
- **Conflict Avoidance:** An inability to express dissenting opinions, set boundaries, or address issues in relationships for fear of rejection or severing the connection.
- **Compromising Personal Values:** Sacrificing your own beliefs, desires, or goals to align with someone else's, believing that this is the only way to maintain the relationship.
- **Clinginess or Neediness:** An intense desire for constant contact, reassurance, or attention from others, which can paradoxically push people away.
- **Tolerating Unhealthy Relationships:** Remaining in relationships that are draining, abusive, or unfulfilling because the fear of being alone outweighs the desire for emotional well-being.

Lack of Self-Awareness and Emotional Literacy: The Blind Spots

Sometimes, emotional dependence isn't rooted in malice or deep trauma, but simply a lack of understanding of one's own inner world.

- **Unrecognized Needs:** If you're not aware of your own emotional needs, you might unconsciously look to others to fill a void you can't even articulate.

- **Difficulty Identifying Emotions:** If you struggle to name or understand your own feelings, you might rely on others to interpret your emotional state or tell you how you should feel.
- **Suppressed Emotions:** If you've been taught to suppress "negative" emotions like anger or sadness, these emotions don't disappear; they often manifest as anxiety, physical symptoms, or a reliance on others to manage feelings you're unwilling to confront yourself.
- **Limited Coping Skills:** If you haven't developed a repertoire of healthy ways to manage stress, discomfort, or difficult emotions, you might default to seeking external comfort or distraction.

Understanding these roots is not about dwelling on the past, but about illuminating the pathways that led you to your current emotional patterns. This awareness is incredibly empowering, as it allows you to consciously choose new paths forward. In the next chapter, we'll explore the tangible **costs** of remaining emotionally dependent, solidifying the motivation to embark on the journey toward inner strength and self-reliance.

Chapter 3: The Cost of Dependence: Recognizing the Chains

Now that we've defined emotional dependence and explored its common origins, it's vital to confront its real-world impact. While emotional dependence might offer a fleeting sense of security or comfort, it comes at a significant cost to your relationships, your self-esteem, your ability to make authentic choices, and your overall well-being. Recognizing these "chains" isn't meant to induce guilt or shame, but rather to illuminate the very real reasons why cultivating emotional independence is not just beneficial, but essential for a truly fulfilling life.

Let's look at the tangible ways emotional dependence can hold you back.

Impact on Relationships: The Unhealthy Dance

Paradoxically, emotional dependence often *harms* the very relationships it seeks to preserve. Instead of fostering genuine connection, it can lead to imbalanced, draining, or even resentful dynamics.

- **Codependency and Enmeshment:** This is perhaps the most significant cost. In codependent relationships, one person's emotional state becomes inextricably linked to another's. You might constantly try to "fix" or "save" your partner, or they might control your emotions. Boundaries become blurred, making it impossible to distinguish your needs and feelings from theirs. This creates an unhealthy cycle where neither person can truly grow independently.
- **Resentment and Burnout:** If you consistently prioritize others' needs over your own (a hallmark of emotional dependence), you'll likely accumulate resentment. The "dependent" person may resent the "independent" person for not meeting all their emotional needs, while the "independent" person may feel drained by the constant demands.
- **Difficulty with Conflict and Authenticity:** Fear of abandonment or disapproval often leads to extreme conflict avoidance. You might suppress your true feelings, avoid difficult conversations, or acquiesce to others' desires to keep the peace. This prevents genuine intimacy, as authentic connection requires both parties to feel safe enough to be themselves, even when disagreeing.
- **Attracting and Tolerating Unhealthy Dynamics:** Because emotional dependence thrives on external validation, it can make you more vulnerable to manipulative or even abusive relationships. If your self-worth is low and you fear being alone, you might tolerate behaviors from others that an emotionally independent person would never accept.
- **Lack of Reciprocity:** Emotionally dependent relationships are often one-sided. You might give excessively without receiving, or constantly take without giving back, leading to imbalances where true partnership struggles to exist.

Erosion of Self-Esteem and Identity: Who Am I Without You?

When your emotional well-being is tied to external sources, your sense of self becomes fragile and permeable.

- **Fluctuating Self-Worth:** Your self-esteem becomes a roller coaster, dictated by external validation. A compliment sends you soaring; a criticism or perceived rejection sends you plummeting. This unstable sense of self makes it hard to build consistent confidence.
- **Loss of Authentic Self:** You might constantly adapt your opinions, interests, and personality to fit in or gain approval. Over time, you lose touch with your genuine desires, values, and passions, asking, "Who am I, really?"
- **Difficulty with Decision-Making:** If you constantly seek external approval, you're less likely to trust your own judgment. Even small decisions can become overwhelming, leading to procrastination, indecisiveness, or always deferring to others. This further erodes self-trust.
- **Fear of Failure and Judgment:** When your worth is external, the fear of making a mistake or being judged by others becomes paralyzing. This can prevent you from taking healthy risks, pursuing new opportunities, or even voicing your opinions.
- **Internalized Critic:** The external voices of disapproval or judgment become internalized, creating a harsh inner critic that constantly undermines your confidence and amplifies self-doubt.

Stifled Personal Growth and Overall Well-being: A Caged Spirit

Emotional dependence puts a significant cap on your personal growth and limits your capacity for true happiness and fulfillment.

- **Limited Resilience:** When your emotional anchor is outside yourself, any shake to that external anchor (a relationship ending, a job loss, criticism) can send you into a spiral. You lack the internal resources to weather life's storms.
- **Unaddressed Needs and Desires:** If you prioritize others' needs or suppress your own emotions, your deepest desires and needs go unfulfilled. This can lead to chronic frustration, emptiness, and a sense of "something missing" in your life.
- **Anxiety and Depression:** The constant worry about pleasing others, the fear of abandonment, and the suppression of authentic feelings can lead to heightened anxiety, chronic stress, and contribute to depressive states.
- **Burnout and Exhaustion:** The emotional labor involved in people-pleasing, constant validation-seeking, and managing others' emotions is incredibly draining. You're constantly expending energy trying to control external factors, leaving little left for yourself.
- **Missed Opportunities:** The fear of stepping out of your comfort zone, or the inability to pursue your own path without external validation, can lead to a life filled with "what ifs" and unfulfilled potential.
- **Superficial Happiness:** When happiness is derived solely from external sources, it's often fleeting and conditional. True, lasting happiness comes from an inner sense of peace and alignment, which emotional dependence undermines.

Recognizing these costs is the first powerful step towards change. It's a wake-up call, a realization that the perceived comfort of dependence is a cage that prevents you from soaring. The journey to emotional independence is about reclaiming your power, your peace, and your authentic self. It's about dismantling these chains so you can build a life of genuine freedom and inner strength.

Part 2: The Pillars of Emotional Independence

Chapter 4: Self-Awareness: The Foundation

You can't change what you don't understand. If emotional independence is the house you're building, then **self-awareness** is the bedrock foundation upon which everything else rests. Without a clear and honest understanding of your inner landscape – your emotions, thoughts, patterns, values, and needs – you'll continue to operate on autopilot, swayed by unconscious triggers and external influences.

This chapter will guide you through the essential practices of cultivating self-awareness, laying the groundwork for all the subsequent pillars of emotional independence.

Understanding Your Emotional Landscape: The Language of Feelings

Emotions are not arbitrary; they are data, signals from your inner world. For an emotionally dependent person, emotions can feel overwhelming or as though they're dictated by external events. Cultivating emotional independence starts with learning to be an observer of your emotions, rather than being controlled by them.

- **Emotional Literacy:** Can you accurately name what you're feeling? Beyond "good" or "bad," can you identify nuances like frustration, contentment, anxiety, excitement, sadness, anger, joy, curiosity? Expanding your emotional vocabulary helps you understand the specific messages your feelings are sending.
  - *Exercise:* The "Emotion Check-In." Several times a day, pause and ask yourself: "What am I feeling right now?" Try to name it without judgment. If it's vague, ask: "What sensation is in my body? What thought is accompanying this feeling?"
- **The Difference Between Emotion, Thought, and Sensation:**
  - **Emotion:** A feeling state (e.g., sadness, joy).
  - **Thought:** A cognitive process (e.g., "I'm not good enough," "This will be great").
  - **Sensation:** A physical experience in the body (e.g., knot in stomach, tightness in chest, warmth). Dependent individuals often conflate these. "I *feel* like you hate me" is a thought, not a feeling. "I *feel* a tightness in my chest and my heart racing" are sensations, often associated with anxiety. Learning to disentangle these helps you respond more skillfully.
- **Identifying Your Triggers:** What external events, specific people, or internal thoughts consistently provoke strong emotional reactions in you?
  - *Example Triggers:* Criticism, feeling ignored, a specific tone of voice, rejection, public speaking, comparison on social media.
  - *Action:* Keep a **"Trigger Journal."** When you have a strong emotional reaction, note:

- What happened just before? (The trigger)
- What emotion did you feel?
- What thoughts went through your mind?
- What sensations did you notice in your body?
- How did you react (or want to react)? This pattern recognition is invaluable for anticipating and managing your responses.

Uncovering Your Core Values: Your Inner Compass

Emotional independence means making choices aligned with *your* authentic self, not someone else's expectations. To do this, you need to know what truly matters to you. Your **core values** are the fundamental beliefs that guide your actions and shape your character. They are your non-negotiables, your deepest motivators.

- **What are Values?** Values are not goals. Goals are destinations; values are the principles that guide your journey. Examples include integrity, compassion, freedom, growth, security, creativity, connection, courage, honesty, adventure.
- **Identifying Your Values:**
  - Think about times you felt truly fulfilled, alive, or proud. What values were being expressed?
  - Think about times you felt angry, frustrated, or deeply uncomfortable. What values were being violated?
  - If money/time were no object, what would you spend your time doing? What would you advocate for?
  - Consider a list of values (easily found online) and highlight the top 5-10 that resonate most deeply.
- **Values in Action:** Once identified, consciously reflect on how your daily choices align (or misalign) with these values. Emotional dependence often leads to actions that betray your values in pursuit of external approval.
  - *Example:* If "integrity" is a core value, but you lie to avoid conflict, that misalignment will cause inner distress. Recognizing this allows you to course-correct.

Understanding Your Needs: Beyond the Superficial

Many emotionally dependent individuals struggle to identify and articulate their own needs, often expecting others to magically fulfill them or suppressing them entirely. Self-awareness involves deeply understanding your own emotional, physical, and psychological needs.

- **Basic Needs:** Beyond Maslow's hierarchy (food, water, shelter), think about your fundamental emotional needs:
  - **Connection:** Do you need social interaction, and what kind?
  - **Autonomy:** Do you need a sense of control over your life choices?
  - **Competence:** Do you need to feel effective and capable?
  - **Safety/Security:** Do you need predictability and emotional safety?
  - **Expression:** Do you need to express your creativity, thoughts, or feelings?
  - **Rest/Recharge:** What truly replenishes your energy?

- **Differentiating Needs from Wants:** A "need" is essential for your well-being. A "want" is a preference. "I need attention" might actually be "I need connection and validation, and attention is how I've learned to seek it." Dig deeper into the underlying need.
- **Journaling Your Needs:** Regularly journal about what you feel you're lacking, what would make you feel more fulfilled, or what brings you true peace. This practice helps you articulate what you need, making it possible to then strategize how to meet those needs for yourself.

Self-awareness is an ongoing practice, not a one-time achievement. It requires curiosity, honesty, and a willingness to look inward without judgment. It's the daily practice of checking in, asking questions, and paying attention to the subtle cues your inner world provides. By mastering self-awareness, you build the unbreakable foundation upon which all other pillars of emotional independence will stand, empowering you to navigate your emotions, live by your values, and meet your own needs.

Chapter 5: Self-Validation: Your Inner Anchor

Once you've built a solid foundation of self-awareness – understanding your emotions, values, and needs – the next critical pillar of emotional independence is **self-validation**. This is the ability to acknowledge, accept, and affirm your own internal experiences (thoughts, feelings, needs, and beliefs) without needing external approval or confirmation.

For someone accustomed to emotional dependence, self-validation can feel revolutionary. It's the shift from constantly looking outward for permission to feel or be, to grounding yourself firmly within your own truth. It's about becoming your own most trusted source of reassurance and worth.

What is Self-Validation (and Why Is It Hard)?

Imagine you're feeling sad.

- **External Validation:** You tell a friend, "I'm sad," hoping they'll say, "It's okay to be sad," or offer solutions. If they don't respond how you expect, your sadness might deepen, or you might question its legitimacy.
- **Self-Validation:** You notice, "I am feeling sad right now. This is a normal human emotion given the circumstances. It's okay to feel this." You acknowledge the feeling without needing anyone else to approve of it or fix it.

Why is self-validation often so challenging?

- **Early Life Conditioning:** Many of us grew up in environments where our feelings were dismissed ("Don't be sad," "Stop crying"), judged ("You're too sensitive," "That's a silly thing to worry about"), or even punished. We learned that certain emotions were "bad" or unacceptable, leading us to suppress them or seek external permission to feel.
- **Societal Pressure for Positivity:** There's a pervasive cultural narrative that we should always be happy, optimistic, or "fine." This can make us feel ashamed of difficult emotions, making us crave external reassurance that it's okay to not be okay.
- **Fear of Being Selfish or Arrogant:** Some people mistakenly equate self-validation with narcissism or selfishness. In reality, it's about self-respect, not self-aggrandizement.
- **Habit of External Locus of Control:** If you're used to others defining your worth or your emotional state, breaking that habit requires conscious effort and trust in your own internal compass.

The Power of Acknowledgment, Not Agreement

Self-validation isn't about agreeing with every thought or acting on every feeling. It's about acknowledging their presence with compassion and non-judgment.

- **Acknowledge the Feeling:** "I feel really angry right now." (Even if you don't like the feeling.)
- **Acknowledge the Thought:** "I'm having the thought that I'm not good enough." (This isn't saying you *are* not good enough, just that you're *having the thought*.)
- **Acknowledge the Need:** "I feel overwhelmed, and I need a break."

- **Acknowledge the Experience:** "That was a really difficult conversation."

The key is to meet your inner experience with empathy, much like a good friend would. You wouldn't tell a friend, "You shouldn't feel that way!" Instead, you'd listen and say, "That sounds really tough." Self-validation applies that same kindness to yourself.

Practices for Cultivating Self-Validation:

1. **Mindful Observation:**
   o **Tune In:** Regularly pause and ask yourself: "What am I experiencing right now, internally?" Notice thoughts, feelings, and physical sensations without judgment.
   o **Name It to Tame It:** Give your emotions a name. Simply labeling a feeling ("This is anxiety," "This is frustration") can reduce its intensity and help you process it.
2. **Validate Your Emotions and Thoughts:**
   o **Use Validating Language:** Talk to yourself as you would a dear friend. Phrases like:
     - "It makes sense that I'm feeling [emotion] given [situation]."
     - "It's okay to feel [emotion]."
     - "I understand why I might be thinking [thought]."
     - "Anyone in my situation might feel this way."
   o **Permission to Feel:** Consciously give yourself permission to feel *any* emotion, even the uncomfortable ones. Emotions are not right or wrong; they simply *are*. Suppressing them only makes them stronger.
   o **Practice Self-Compassion:** When you're struggling, offer yourself kindness instead of criticism. Put a hand on your heart, take a deep breath, and acknowledge your pain.
3. **Journaling for Self-Validation:**
   o **The "Feelings & Validation" Log:**
     - *What happened?* (Briefly describe the situation.)
     - *What did I feel?* (Name the emotions and sensations.)
     - *What thoughts did I have?* (Write down your inner dialogue.)
     - *My Self-Validation:* (Write down compassionate, non-judgmental statements affirming your experience. For example: "It's understandable that I felt angry when my boundaries were crossed," or "It makes sense that I'm worried about this, as it's an important decision.")
4. **Embracing Imperfection:**
   o Understand that self-validation extends to your flaws and mistakes. You are a human being, not a perfect robot. When you make a mistake, validate the effort, the learning, and your humanity, rather than diving into self-criticism. "I messed up there, and that's hard, but I'm learning, and that's part of growth."
5. **Reducing External Validation Seeking:**
   o Consciously identify times when you're about to seek external validation (e.g., constantly asking "Am I doing okay?", fishing for compliments, needing someone else to confirm your decision).
   o Before you ask, pause. Can you offer that validation to yourself first? Can you trust your own judgment? This isn't about *never* asking for feedback, but about not *needing* it to feel secure.

Self-validation is the muscle that allows you to stand firm in your own truth, even when the world outside is chaotic or unsupportive. It's the inner "yes" that tells you, "I am here, I am real, and my experience matters." As you develop this inner anchor, you'll find that external opinions hold less power, difficult emotions become more manageable, and your sense of self becomes unshakably secure. This inner strength is what truly frees you to engage with the world from a place of wholeness, rather than need.

Chapter 6: Self-Responsibility: Owning Your Narrative

With self-awareness as your foundation and self-validation as your anchor, the next crucial pillar of emotional independence is **self-responsibility**. This means taking ownership of your choices, your reactions, and your emotional well-being, rather than placing the burden on external circumstances or other people.

For someone who has been emotionally dependent, this can be a challenging but incredibly liberating shift. It's moving from a mindset of "this is happening *to* me" to "I have agency in how I respond to what's happening." It's about recognizing that while you can't control everything, you *can* control your inner world and your actions.

What is Self-Responsibility in the Emotional Realm?

Self-responsibility is not about blaming yourself for everything that goes wrong. It's about acknowledging your part in your experiences and empowering yourself to make changes.

- **Emotional Ownership:** Understanding that your emotions are *yours*. While external events can trigger them, *you* are responsible for how you process and respond to those feelings.
- **Choice in Response:** Recognizing that you have a choice in how you react to people and situations, rather than being a passive recipient of external stimuli.
- **Beyond Blame:** Shifting away from blaming others or circumstances for your unhappiness, and instead, asking "What can *I* do about this?"
- **Meeting Your Own Needs:** Taking proactive steps to identify and fulfill your own needs, rather than expecting others to instinctively know and meet them for you.
- **Accountability for Actions:** Holding yourself accountable for the consequences of your choices, both positive and negative.

The Difference Between Blame and Responsibility

This distinction is critical:

- **Blame:** Assigning fault to someone or something outside yourself for a negative outcome. Blame keeps you stuck and disempowered. "I'm unhappy because my partner doesn't understand me."
- **Responsibility:** Acknowledging your role, your choices, and your capacity to respond. Responsibility empowers you to act. "I'm unhappy in this dynamic. What can *I* do to communicate my needs differently, or what choices do I need to make for my well-being?"

An emotionally independent person understands that while others may contribute to a situation, their own response and choices are ultimately their responsibility.

1. **Shift Your Language:**
   - **From "You make me feel..." to "I feel... when...":** Instead of "You make me angry when you do that," try "I feel angry when that happens, and I need to address it." This subtle shift places the feeling back on you and opens the door for internal processing, rather than external accusation.
   - **From "I have to..." to "I choose to...":** "I have to go to this event" becomes "I choose to go to this event because..." This reclaims your agency.
   - **From "If only..." to "What now?":** Instead of dwelling on what could have been, focus on actionable steps.

2. **Embrace the "Locus of Control" Concept:**
   - **Internal Locus of Control:** Believing that you are primarily in control of your own life and outcomes. Emotionally independent people lean towards this.
   - **External Locus of Control:** Believing that outside forces (fate, luck, other people) primarily determine your life's outcomes. Emotional dependence often stems from this.
   - **Action:** Consciously challenge thoughts that assign all power to external forces. For every "I can't because they...", ask "What *can* I do, regardless of them?" Focus your energy on what is within your sphere of influence.

3. **Practice Mindful Response, Not Reaction:**
   - When faced with a trigger or a difficult situation, pause. Instead of an immediate, habitual reaction (which is often fear-based or externally driven), take a breath. Ask yourself:
     - "What emotion am I feeling?" (Self-awareness)
     - "Is this feeling valid?" (Self-validation)
     - "What is my desired outcome here?"
     - "What response aligns with my values and long-term well-being?"
   - This pause creates space for a conscious, responsible choice.

4. **Take Action to Meet Your Own Needs:**
   - Based on the self-awareness you cultivated in Chapter 4, identify a need that you've been neglecting or expecting others to fulfill.
   - Then, actively make a plan to meet that need yourself.
     - *Example:* If you need more intellectual stimulation, don't wait for someone to suggest a book club. Join one, or start reading that non-fiction book you've been eyeing.
     - *Example:* If you need more alone time, intentionally schedule it into your week, even if it means saying "no" to a social invitation.
   - This proactive approach reinforces your capacity to care for yourself.

5. **Learn from Your Mistakes (Without Blame):**
   - When something goes wrong, instead of getting caught in a loop of self-blame or blaming others, engage in reflective learning.
   - Ask: "What was my part in this?" "What could I have done differently?" "What did I learn from this experience?"

- o This is constructive self-responsibility that leads to growth, rather than destructive blame that leads to paralysis.
6. **Set Realistic Expectations:**
   - o Acknowledge that you are human and will make mistakes. Self-responsibility is not about being perfect, but about being accountable for your continued learning and growth.
   - o Also, be responsible in your expectations of others. You cannot expect others to fulfill all your needs; that's your job.

Embracing self-responsibility is arguably the most powerful step towards emotional independence. It moves you from a passive passenger to the conscious driver of your life. It means accepting the full scope of your power to choose, to respond, and to shape your emotional world. This newfound agency transforms victimhood into empowerment, paving the way for truly authentic living.

Chapter 7: Healthy Boundaries: Protecting Your Space

With self-awareness, self-validation, and self-responsibility firmly established, the final and arguably most tangible pillar of emotional independence is the ability to create and maintain **healthy boundaries**. Boundaries are essentially the invisible lines we draw to protect our physical, emotional, and energetic space. They define what you are and are not comfortable with, what you will and will not accept, and what is your responsibility versus someone else's.

For someone striving for emotional independence, boundaries are non-negotiable. Without them, the self you are building becomes permeable, allowing external influences to easily intrude and undermine your inner stability. They are the ultimate expression of self-care and respect.

What Are Boundaries and Why Are They Essential?

Think of boundaries like the fence around your home. It's not there to keep everyone out, but to define your property, protect your privacy, and allow you to decide who gets in and under what conditions.

Healthy boundaries are crucial because they:

- **Protect Your Emotional Energy:** They prevent you from becoming drained by other people's problems, demands, or negativity.
- **Define Your Identity:** They clarify where you end and others begin, reinforcing your separate sense of self.
- **Communicate Your Needs:** They are a direct way of telling others what you need to feel safe, respected, and comfortable.
- **Foster Respect:** When you respect your own boundaries, others are more likely to respect them too.
- **Enable Authentic Connection:** True intimacy thrives where both parties feel safe enough to be themselves and respect each other's individuality. Unhealthy boundaries lead to resentment and enmeshment.
- **Reduce Resentment:** When your boundaries are consistently violated, resentment builds. Setting them reduces this friction.
- **Promote Self-Care:** Setting boundaries is a fundamental act of self-care, ensuring you prioritize your well-being.

Common Types of Boundaries:

Boundaries aren't just about saying "no." They encompass various aspects of your life:

1. **Physical Boundaries:** Your personal space, touch, and physical belongings. (e.g., "Please don't touch my hair without asking," "I'm not comfortable with hugs right now.")
2. **Time Boundaries:** How you allocate your time and energy. (e.g., "I can meet for coffee, but only for an hour," "I don't check work emails after 6 PM.")
3. **Emotional Boundaries:** What emotional information you will and won't take on from others, and how you choose to engage with emotional intensity. (e.g., "I can listen to your

problem, but I can't solve it for you," "I need to take a break from this conversation; it's too intense.")

4. **Mental/Intellectual Boundaries:** Your thoughts, opinions, and beliefs. Respecting others' right to their own thoughts and expecting the same in return. (e.g., "I understand you have a different opinion, but I won't debate this topic," "Please don't tell me what I should think.")

5. **Material/Financial Boundaries:** Your money and possessions. (e.g., "I'm not lending money right now," "Please ask before you borrow my car.")

Why Setting Boundaries Is Hard (Especially for the Dependent):

For those prone to emotional dependence, setting boundaries can feel terrifying because it triggers core fears:

- **Fear of Rejection/Abandonment:** "If I say no, they won't like me/will leave me."
- **Fear of Conflict:** "It's easier to just go along with it than to deal with an argument."
- **Guilt:** "I feel guilty saying no, especially if they need me."
- **Belief of Selfishness:** "Setting a boundary means I'm being selfish."
- **Lack of Practice:** If you've never done it, it feels awkward and unfamiliar.
- **Uncertainty of Your Own Needs:** If you're not self-aware, it's hard to know what boundaries you need.

Practices for Cultivating Healthy Boundaries:

1. **Identify Your Boundaries:**
   o **Reflect on Resentment:** Where do you feel resentful, drained, or taken advantage of? These are often indicators that a boundary is needed.
   o **Listen to Your "No" Signals:** Pay attention to that knot in your stomach, the tension in your shoulders, or the inner voice that says, "I don't want to do this." These are your internal boundary alarms.
   o **List Your Non-Negotiables:** What are the absolute limits beyond which you will not go? What are your deal-breakers?

2. **Start Small and Practice:**
   o Don't try to overhaul all your boundaries at once. Pick one area where you feel relatively safe and start there.
   o *Example:* If you always feel obligated to answer calls immediately, practice letting it go to voicemail and calling back when *you're* ready.

3. **Communicate Clearly and Concisely:**
   o **Be Direct, Not Aggressive:** Use "I" statements. "I'm not available to help with that right now" is better than "You always ask too much of me."
   o **Be Brief and Firm:** You don't need to over-explain or justify your boundary. "No, thank you." is often sufficient. "I appreciate you asking, but I won't be able to."
   o **State What You WILL Do (if applicable):** "I can't do X, but I can do Y." This offers an alternative without caving on your boundary.

4. **Expect Pushback (It's Normal!):**
   - When you start setting boundaries, especially with people accustomed to your lack of them, they might react with surprise, confusion, anger, or guilt-tripping. This is a test.
   - **Stay Calm and Consistent:** Reiterate your boundary calmly. "I understand you're disappointed, but my answer remains no."
   - **Their Reaction Isn't Your Responsibility:** Their emotional reaction is *their* responsibility, not yours. Your responsibility is to uphold your boundary.
5. **Differentiate Between Boundaries and Walls:**
   - **Boundaries:** Are about protecting your space and energy to allow for healthier, more authentic connection. They are flexible and allow for give-and-take.
   - **Walls:** Are rigid barriers that prevent connection and keep everyone out. They are born of fear and can lead to isolation.
   - The goal is boundaries, not walls.
6. **Practice Saying "No":**
   - "No, thank you."
   - "I appreciate the offer, but I can't."
   - "That doesn't work for me."
   - "I need to prioritize something else right now."

Setting and maintaining healthy boundaries is an ongoing process that requires courage and self-compassion. It will feel uncomfortable at first, but with practice, it becomes empowering. Each time you successfully uphold a boundary, you reinforce your self-worth, strengthen your inner anchor, and move further along the path to true emotional independence. You're not just saying "no" to others; you're saying a resounding "yes" to yourself.

Part 3: Cultivating Inner Strength

Chapter 8: Managing Your Emotions

With the foundational pillars in place, we can now turn our attention to actively cultivating the inner strength that allows you to thrive as an emotionally independent individual. A cornerstone of this strength is the ability to **manage your emotions effectively**. This doesn't mean suppressing or ignoring your feelings; it means learning to experience, understand, and navigate them in a way that serves your well-being, rather than being overwhelmed or controlled by them.

For those prone to emotional dependence, emotions can feel like a turbulent sea, often dictated by external winds. Emotional management is about learning to sail your own ship, even in a storm, rather than being tossed around by every wave.

The Myth of "Controlling" Emotions:

Let's clear this up immediately: you cannot truly "control" your emotions in the sense of turning them on and off like a light switch. Emotions are automatic, physiological responses to internal or external stimuli. Trying to suppress them is often counterproductive and can lead to emotional backlog, anxiety, and even physical symptoms.

Instead of control, the goal is **regulation** and **wise response**. This means:

- **Awareness:** Knowing what you're feeling (from Chapter 4).
- **Acceptance:** Allowing the feeling to be there without judgment (from Chapter 5).
- **Understanding:** Recognizing the message the emotion is sending (from Chapter 4).
- **Processing:** Moving through the emotion in a healthy way.
- **Responding Wisely:** Choosing your actions based on your values, rather than impulsively reacting to the emotion.

Strategies for Emotional Regulation:

1. **The "STOP" Skill (DBT-inspired):** This is a powerful, quick technique for managing intense emotions in the moment:
   - **S - Stop:** Whatever you're doing, just stop. Don't react. Don't say anything. Don't move.
   - **T - Take a Breath:** Take several slow, deep breaths. This activates your parasympathetic nervous system, helping to calm your body.
   - **O - Observe:** Notice what's happening internally (thoughts, feelings, sensations) and externally (the situation). Detach slightly and just observe without judgment.
   - **P - Proceed with Purpose:** After this brief pause, choose your next action mindfully, aligning with your goals and values, rather than reacting impulsively.
2. **Emotional Grounding Techniques:** When emotions feel overwhelming, grounding helps bring you back to the present moment and your physical body.
   - **5-4-3-2-1 Method:** Name 5 things you can see, 4 things you can feel, 3 things you can hear, 2 things you can smell, and 1 thing you can taste.

- o **Tactile Grounding:** Hold a comforting object, notice the texture of your clothes, or place your feet firmly on the floor and feel the sensation.
- o **Mindful Breathing:** Focus intently on the sensation of your breath entering and leaving your body. Count your breaths.
3. **Process, Don't Suppress:** Emotions need an outlet. Healthy processing allows them to move through you.
    - o **Journaling:** Writing down your feelings, thoughts, and what triggered them is incredibly cathartic. Don't censor yourself.
    - o **Talking to a Trusted Person:** Share your feelings with someone who can listen without judgment or trying to "fix" you. (Ensure this is for processing, not external validation.)
    - o **Physical Release:** Intense emotions like anger or anxiety can benefit from physical movement:
        - Exercise (running, dancing, hitting a punching bag)
        - Screaming into a pillow
        - Punching or kneading dough
    - o **Creative Expression:** Draw, paint, play music, or write poetry to express what words cannot.
4. **Challenge Distorted Thinking (Cognitive Reappraisal):**
    - o Our thoughts often fuel our emotions. Emotionally dependent individuals often fall into cognitive distortions (e.g., catastrophizing, black-and-white thinking, mind-reading).
    - o When you notice an intense emotion, ask yourself:
        - "What thoughts am I having right now?"
        - "Is this thought 100% true? Are there other ways to interpret this situation?"
        - "Am I jumping to conclusions or assuming the worst?"
        - "What would a rational, compassionate person think in this situation?"
        - "Is this thought serving me?"
    - o Gently reframe negative or unhelpful thoughts. For example, instead of "They hate me," try "They seem busy, and I'm feeling a bit insecure."
5. **Develop a "Self-Soothing Toolkit":**
    - o What activities genuinely comfort and calm you when you're distressed? Make a list and actively engage in them.
    - o *Examples:* Listening to calming music, taking a warm bath, drinking a favorite tea, reading a book, spending time in nature, cuddling a pet, practicing gentle yoga.
    - o These are *not* distractions to avoid feelings, but intentional ways to soothe yourself through them.
6. **Practice Emotional Detox (When Necessary):**
    - o Sometimes, managing emotions means temporarily stepping away from their source.
    - o Take a "time out" from a stressful conversation.
    - o Limit exposure to news or social media that triggers overwhelming emotions.
    - o Spend time with people who uplift you, rather than those who drain you.

Learning to manage your emotions is an ongoing skill, not a destination. It requires patience, practice, and self-compassion. The more you practice these strategies, the more adept you become at navigating your inner world, fostering a sense of inner peace, and confidently moving through life's emotional currents as an emotionally independent individual. You learn that feelings, even difficult ones, are temporary visitors, not permanent residents, and you have the power to influence their stay.

Chapter 9: Developing Self-Trust and Confidence

Building on the ability to manage your emotions, a crucial component of inner strength for emotional independence is the cultivation of **self-trust and confidence**. These aren't abstract concepts; they are the direct result of consistently relying on your own judgment, honoring your commitments to yourself, and acting in alignment with your values. For those who've leaned on external validation, shifting this reliance inward is a profound and liberating experience.

Self-trust is the quiet knowing that you can handle what life throws at you, and confidence is the outward expression of that inner assurance. They empower you to make decisions from a place of inner knowing, rather than second-guessing yourself or seeking endless external affirmation.

The Interplay of Self-Trust and Confidence:

- **Self-Trust is the Foundation:** It's the belief in your own reliability, your capacity to make good choices, and your ability to follow through on your intentions. You trust your instincts and your inner compass.
- **Confidence is the Outcome:** When you trust yourself, you naturally exude confidence. This isn't arrogance, but a calm assurance in your abilities and your worth, regardless of external outcomes.

Lack of self-trust often manifests as chronic indecision, seeking excessive advice, people-pleasing, or a fear of making mistakes. When you don't trust yourself, you hand that trust over to others, becoming emotionally dependent.

Practices for Cultivating Self-Trust and Confidence:

1. **Start Small and Build Momentum (The "Trust Bank" Account):**
   - Think of self-trust like a bank account. Every time you follow through on a commitment to yourself, you make a deposit. Every time you break a promise to yourself, you make a withdrawal.
   - **Action:** Begin with small, achievable promises.
     - "I will go for a 15-minute walk today."
     - "I will spend 10 minutes meditating."
     - "I will respond to that email within the hour."
     - "I will say 'no' to one non-essential request this week."
   - Consistently keeping these small promises builds a strong sense of self-reliability. You prove to yourself, repeatedly, "I can count on me."
2. **Practice Mindful Decision-Making:**
   - For everyday decisions, consciously try to make choices based on your own internal compass, rather than immediately seeking external input.
   - **The "Pause and Consult Yourself" Method:**
     - **Identify the decision:** Big or small.
     - **Pause:** Take a few deep breaths.
     - **Consult your intuition:** What does your gut tell you? What feels right for *you*?

- **Consider your values:** Does this decision align with your core values (from Chapter 4)?
- **Weigh the pros and cons (briefly):** Don't over-analyze, but consider practical aspects.
- **Decide and Act:** Commit to your decision and move forward.
  - Even if the outcome isn't "perfect," the *act* of making the decision independently builds self-trust. You learn that you are capable of navigating choices.

3. **Embrace and Learn from Mistakes:**
   - A significant barrier to self-trust is the fear of failure or making the "wrong" decision. Shift your perspective from perfection to **learning and growth**.
   - When you make a mistake, instead of self-criticism, ask: "What did I learn from this? What can I do differently next time?"
   - *Self-Trust Affirmation:* "Even if I make a mistake, I trust my ability to learn, adapt, and move forward." This reframes mistakes as data points for growth, not evidence of inadequacy.

4. **Acknowledge Your Strengths and Accomplishments:**
   - Emotionally dependent individuals often downplay their strengths and focus on their weaknesses, relying on others to highlight their positive attributes.
   - **Action:** Keep a "Wins Journal" or a "Strength List."
     - Regularly write down your accomplishments, big or small.
     - List your unique skills, talents, and positive qualities.
     - Refer back to this list when self-doubt creeps in.
   - This practice helps you internalize your capabilities and build genuine confidence from within.

5. **Set and Uphold Boundaries (Reinforce Trust):**
   - As discussed in Chapter 7, boundaries are crucial. When you set and maintain a boundary, you are signaling to yourself, "My needs and my space are important, and I will protect them." This builds immense self-trust and reinforces your personal power.
   - Breaking your own boundaries, conversely, erodes self-trust.

6. **Practice Positive Self-Talk:**
   - Your inner dialogue profoundly impacts your self-trust and confidence. Challenge the negative, critical voice.
   - **Replace negative self-talk with supportive self-talk:**
     - Instead of "I'm going to mess this up," try "I'll do my best, and I can handle whatever happens."
     - Instead of "I'm not good enough," try "I am capable, and I'm learning."
   - Treat yourself with the same encouragement and belief you'd offer to a loved one.

7. **Take Intentional Risks:**
   - Stepping outside your comfort zone, even in small ways, builds confidence by proving to yourself that you can handle discomfort and uncertainty.
   - *Examples:* Trying a new hobby, speaking up in a meeting, traveling alone, initiating a difficult conversation.
   - The act of taking the risk, regardless of the outcome, reinforces your courage and competence.

Developing self-trust and confidence is a continuous journey of proving to yourself, through consistent action and compassionate self-talk, that you are reliable, capable, and worthy. As this inner conviction grows, the need for external validation diminishes, allowing you to walk through life with a quiet strength and an unshakeable belief in yourself. This is where true inner strength takes root.

Chapter 10: Embracing Solitude and Self-Discovery

One of the most profound markers of emotional independence is the ability to not just tolerate, but actively **embrace solitude**. For those accustomed to emotional dependence, the idea of being alone can trigger anxiety, loneliness, or a pervasive sense of emptiness. However, solitude is not the same as loneliness; it is a powerful space for **self-discovery**, introspection, and true inner replenishment.

This chapter will guide you in reframing solitude from a void to be filled, into a fertile ground for growth, creativity, and deeper connection with your authentic self. It is in this space that you truly learn who you are when no one else is watching, and what genuinely brings you peace and joy.

Solitude vs. Loneliness: A Crucial Distinction

- **Loneliness** is an emotional state characterized by a feeling of emptiness, isolation, or longing for connection, even when surrounded by others. It's often a painful experience stemming from a perceived lack of meaningful social interaction.
- **Solitude** is a chosen state of being alone, intentionally setting aside time for oneself without external distractions or social obligations. It's a positive, enriching experience that allows for introspection, creativity, and self-recharge.

An emotionally dependent person often confuses these two, fearing solitude because it brings up feelings of loneliness. An emotionally independent person recognizes the difference and actively seeks out healthy solitude to nourish their inner world.

The Transformative Power of Solitude:

Embracing solitude offers immense benefits for emotional independence:

- **Deeper Self-Awareness:** Without external input, you can hear your own thoughts, feelings, and needs more clearly. It's an opportunity to truly listen to your inner voice.
- **Enhanced Creativity:** Many artists, writers, and innovators find their best ideas emerge during periods of uninterrupted solitude. It allows for divergent thinking and exploration.
- **Emotional Processing:** It provides space to process difficult emotions, reflect on experiences, and integrate learning without external distractions or pressures to "perform" emotionally.
- **Self-Replenishment:** Social interaction, even positive interaction, can be draining. Solitude offers a chance to recharge your social and emotional batteries.
- **Clarity of Values and Goals:** Away from external influences, you can reconnect with your core values and gain clarity on your true desires and life direction.
- **Developing Self-Sufficiency:** It builds confidence in your ability to be content and resourceful in your own company, proving that your happiness doesn't depend on others.

1. **Schedule "Me Time" Deliberately:**
   - Treat your solitude like any other important appointment. Start small: 15-30 minutes a day, then gradually increase.
   - This could be a quiet morning coffee, a walk in nature, or simply sitting in a room by yourself without your phone.
   - **Action:** Block out specific times in your calendar for uninterrupted solo activities.
2. **Disconnect from Digital Distractions:**
   - True solitude requires minimizing digital noise. Put your phone on airplane mode, turn off notifications, and step away from social media.
   - The constant pull of digital connection can prevent you from truly being present with yourself.
3. **Engage in Solo Activities You Enjoy:**
   - What brings *you* joy when you're alone? Explore hobbies and activities that are intrinsically motivating and don't require external validation.
   - *Examples:* Reading, gardening, painting, hiking, listening to music, cooking a new recipe, journaling, meditating, playing an instrument, doing a puzzle.
   - The goal is to find activities that genuinely absorb you and bring a sense of flow and contentment.
4. **Practice Mindful Reflection and Journaling:**
   - Use your time alone to actively reflect. Ask yourself powerful questions:
     - "What am I truly feeling right now?"
     - "What do I need in this moment?"
     - "What am I grateful for?"
     - "What ideas am I excited about?"
     - "What have I learned recently?"
   - Journaling is an excellent tool for this; it provides a private, non-judgmental space for your thoughts and emotions.
5. **Reframe "Alone" as "Whole":**
   - Consciously challenge the negative connotations you might have with being alone. Replace thoughts like "I'm so alone" with "I am whole within myself," or "I am enjoying my own company."
   - Focus on the *quality* of your solitude, not the quantity of people around you.
6. **Spend Time in Nature:**
   - Nature is a powerful ally for self-discovery and inner peace. Take solo walks, sit by a lake, or simply observe the sky. The vastness and quiet of nature can help you feel grounded and connected to something larger than yourself.
7. **Explore Your Inner World (Meditation/Mindfulness):**
   - Even short periods of mindfulness meditation can deepen your connection to your inner self. Sit quietly and simply observe your breath, thoughts, and sensations without judgment.
   - This practice trains your mind to be present with yourself, reducing the need for external stimulation.

Embracing solitude is a courageous act of self-love and a cornerstone of emotional independence. It teaches you that your happiness is not contingent on the presence of others, but rather on the richness of your inner life. As you cultivate comfort and joy in your own company, you become a more resilient, authentic, and truly independent individual, ready to engage with the world from a place of abundance.

Chapter 11: Resilience in the Face of Adversity

Life is inherently unpredictable, filled with challenges, setbacks, and disappointments. For an emotionally dependent person, adversity can feel catastrophic, often leading to overwhelm, despair, and a desperate search for external comfort or rescue. For the emotionally independent individual, however, adversity is met with **resilience** – the remarkable ability to bounce back, adapt, and even grow stronger in the face of difficulties.

This chapter is about cultivating that inner fortitude, understanding that while you cannot control external events, you absolutely can control your response to them. Resilience is not about avoiding pain; it's about navigating it with strength, learning, and an unwavering belief in your capacity to endure and thrive.

What is Resilience? More Than Just Bouncing Back

Resilience is often described as "bouncing back," but it's more than that. It's a dynamic process that involves:

- **Adaptability:** The ability to adjust to new circumstances and find new ways of functioning when old methods no longer work.
- **Growth:** Emerging from difficult experiences stronger, wiser, and with new perspectives.
- **Self-Efficacy:** A belief in your own ability to succeed in specific situations or to accomplish a task.
- **Problem-Solving:** The capacity to identify issues and find effective solutions.
- **Emotional Regulation:** Managing stress and negative emotions in healthy ways (as discussed in Chapter 8).

Resilience doesn't mean you don't feel pain, sadness, or anger. It means you don't get stuck in those feelings, and you have the internal resources to move through them effectively.

The Link Between Emotional Independence and Resilience:

The pillars of emotional independence directly contribute to resilience:

- **Self-Awareness:** Allows you to identify your emotional state and triggers during adversity.
- **Self-Validation:** Enables you to accept difficult emotions without judgment, preventing suppression that can hinder recovery.
- **Self-Responsibility:** Empowers you to take agency in your response, rather than feeling like a victim of circumstances.
- **Healthy Boundaries:** Protects your energy and prevents you from being overwhelmed by external stressors or the emotional burdens of others.
- **Self-Trust and Confidence:** Gives you the belief that you can overcome challenges and trust your own judgment in difficult times.
- **Embracing Solitude:** Provides the necessary space for reflection, emotional processing, and inner replenishment after a challenging event.

Practices for Cultivating Resilience:

1. **Develop a Growth Mindset:**
   - This is a fundamental shift. Instead of viewing challenges as insurmountable obstacles or failures as definitive endpoints, see them as **opportunities for learning and growth**.
   - *Action:* When faced with a setback, ask: "What can I learn from this? How can this experience make me stronger or wiser?" Focus on the process of becoming, rather than the outcome.
2. **Practice Realistic Optimism:**
   - Resilience isn't about ignoring reality or being Pollyannaish. It's about maintaining a hopeful and realistic outlook.
   - Acknowledge the difficulty, but focus on what you *can* control and the potential for positive outcomes or adaptation.
   - *Action:* Identify worst-case scenarios, but then also identify best-case scenarios and, most importantly, realistic, actionable steps you can take.
3. **Build Your Coping Toolkit (Proactive & Reactive):**
   - Proactively develop a range of healthy coping mechanisms *before* adversity strikes.
   - *Examples:* Exercise, mindfulness, hobbies, spending time in nature, creative expression, connecting with supportive friends (not for dependence, but for connection).
   - During adversity, consciously choose from your toolkit rather than defaulting to unhealthy patterns (e.g., isolation, overeating, excessive escapism).
4. **Cultivate a Sense of Purpose and Meaning:**
   - Having a clear sense of purpose or something larger than yourself to believe in can provide immense strength during difficult times. It gives you a "why" to keep going.
   - *Action:* Reflect on your core values (Chapter 4). How can you live those values even in challenging circumstances? What positive impact do you want to have?
5. **Strengthen Your Problem-Solving Skills:**
   - Resilient individuals don't just endure; they actively seek solutions.
   - *Action:* When faced with a problem:
     - Clearly define the problem.
     - Brainstorm multiple solutions (no judgment).
     - Evaluate the pros and cons of each.
     - Choose a course of action and try it.
     - Review and adjust as needed.
   - This systematic approach replaces feeling helpless with feeling empowered.
6. **Seek Supportive (Not Dependent) Connections:**
   - While emotional independence means not *needing* others for your well-being, healthy, supportive relationships are a vital component of resilience.
   - *Action:* Identify individuals who offer genuine support, encouragement, and a listening ear, without fostering dependence. Be willing to ask for help when needed, but always from a place of agency, not helplessness.
7. **Practice Self-Compassion During Adversity:**
   - When struggling, avoid self-criticism. Treat yourself with the same kindness and understanding you would offer a friend who is suffering.

- *Action:* Acknowledge your pain, remind yourself that suffering is part of the human experience, and offer yourself comfort. "This is hard. It's okay to feel this. I am doing my best."

Resilience is not a trait you either have or don't; it's a dynamic set of skills that can be learned and strengthened over time. By consciously applying the principles of emotional independence, you build an unshakeable inner core that allows you to navigate life's inevitable storms, not just survive them, but emerge with greater wisdom, strength, and a deeper appreciation for your own powerful capacity to thrive.

Part 4: Relationships and Emotional Independence

Chapter 12: Independent Together: Healthy Relationships

One of the biggest misconceptions about emotional independence is that it leads to isolation or a lack of meaningful connection. Nothing could be further from the truth. In fact, emotional independence is the bedrock upon which truly **healthy, vibrant, and authentic relationships** are built. When you are whole within yourself, you enter relationships not from a place of desperate need or fear, but from a place of abundance and genuine choice.

This chapter will explore how emotional independence transforms your interactions, allowing you to form deeper, more fulfilling bonds that honor both your individuality and your shared connection.

The Paradox of Independence in Connection:

It might seem counterintuitive, but the more independent you become, the more capable you are of true intimacy.

- **From Need to Choice:** When you're emotionally dependent, you *need* relationships to feel complete, valued, or secure. This neediness can create pressure, resentment, and an unhealthy dynamic. When you're emotionally independent, you *choose* relationships because they add joy, growth, and companionship to an already rich life. This choice breeds appreciation and genuine connection.
- **From Enmeshment to Interdependence:** Dependent relationships often lead to enmeshment, where identities blur and boundaries dissolve. Healthy relationships are **interdependent**. This means both individuals are autonomous and self-sufficient, but they also rely on and support each other, sharing vulnerabilities and celebrating strengths. It's a dance between "I" and "we."
- **From Control to Freedom:** Dependence often involves attempts to control or manipulate others to meet your emotional needs. Independence fosters a sense of freedom for both parties. You allow your loved ones to be themselves, and they allow you the same grace.

Hallmarks of Independent Relationships:

How do you recognize a relationship where emotional independence thrives?

1. **Clear and Respected Boundaries:** As discussed in Chapter 7, boundaries are essential. Both partners understand and respect each other's emotional, physical, time, and mental limits. There's no guilt for saying "no" or taking space.
2. **Authentic Self-Expression:** Both individuals feel safe enough to express their true thoughts, feelings, and needs without fear of judgment, rejection, or needing to censor themselves to maintain harmony.
3. **Mutual Respect and Support for Growth:** Partners encourage each other's individual growth, passions, and personal development, even if it means temporary time apart or pursuing separate interests. There's no holding each other back.

4. **Shared Responsibility for Happiness:** Each person takes responsibility for their own emotional well-being and happiness. While they offer support, they don't expect their partner to "make" them happy or fix all their problems.
5. **Healthy Conflict Resolution:** Disagreements are seen as opportunities for deeper understanding, not threats to the relationship. Both parties can voice their perspectives, actively listen, and work towards solutions respectfully, without resorting to blame or manipulation.
6. **Quality Over Quantity of Time:** Time spent together is intentional and meaningful, not simply filling a void. There's comfort in both shared activities and individual pursuits.
7. **Strong Sense of Individual Identity:** Both partners maintain a strong sense of who they are outside the relationship – their own friends, hobbies, goals, and values.

Practices for Building Independent Relationships:

1. **Prioritize Your Own Well-being:**
   - Continue to practice self-care, honor your boundaries, and pursue your individual passions. When you're well-resourced, you bring your best self to the relationship.
   - Don't abandon your "me time" or hobbies just because you're in a relationship.
2. **Communicate Your Needs, Don't Expect Them to Be Guessed:**
   - Instead of waiting for your partner to intuit your needs (a common dependent behavior), clearly and calmly articulate what you need using "I" statements.
   - *Example:* "I'm feeling a bit overwhelmed and need some quiet time this evening" vs. silently fuming or acting passive-aggressive.
3. **Encourage and Celebrate Your Partner's Independence:**
   - Support your partner's goals, hobbies, and friendships outside of your shared life. See their individual fulfillment as a positive, not a threat.
   - Acknowledge and affirm their efforts to grow and develop personally.
4. **Practice Active Listening Without Taking Responsibility:**
   - When your partner shares a challenge, listen with empathy and validate their feelings ("That sounds really tough," "I can understand why you'd feel that way").
   - Resist the urge to immediately "fix" it or take on their emotional burden unless specifically asked. Your role is to be a supportive listener, not their emotional savior.
5. **Be Willing to Disagree Respectfully:**
   - True connection doesn't mean always agreeing. It means you can have differing opinions and still maintain respect and love.
   - Learn constructive conflict resolution skills: focus on the issue, not the person; use "I" statements; take breaks when emotions run too high.
6. **Recognize and Address Codependent Tendencies:**
   - If you notice yourself people-pleasing, constantly sacrificing your needs, or feeling responsible for your partner's emotions, gently redirect.
   - Ask: "Is this action coming from a place of genuine care and choice, or from fear/need?"
7. **Foster Shared Experiences AND Individual Experiences:**
   - Actively cultivate shared activities and quality time that strengthen your bond.

- Equally important, create space for individual pursuits and experiences. This balance keeps the relationship fresh and allows both individuals to bring new perspectives and energy back to the partnership.

Relationships built on emotional independence are not devoid of vulnerability or deep connection. Instead, they are richer, more authentic, and more resilient. They are partnerships between two whole individuals who choose to walk together, supporting each other's journeys while maintaining their own unique paths. This is the ultimate expression of love and respect – allowing each other the freedom to be fully ourselves, together.

Chapter 13: Navigating Conflict with Autonomy

Conflict is an inevitable part of any relationship. For the emotionally dependent individual, conflict is often a terrifying prospect, signaling potential rejection or abandonment. This fear can lead to extreme people-pleasing, suppression of true feelings, or passive-aggressive behaviors, all of which erode genuine connection.

For the emotionally independent person, **conflict is seen as an opportunity for growth and deeper understanding**, not a threat. It's about navigating disagreements with autonomy, meaning you approach them from a place of self-respect, clear boundaries, and a commitment to authentic communication, rather than fear or control.

The Fear of Conflict and Its Roots in Dependence:

The intense aversion to conflict in emotionally dependent patterns stems from:

- **Conditional Love:** If early experiences taught you that expressing anger or disagreement risked losing love or approval, you learned to avoid conflict at all costs.
- **Fear of Abandonment:** The ultimate consequence of conflict, in a dependent mindset, is often perceived as total rejection or the end of the relationship.
- **Blurring of Identity:** If your identity is intertwined with another person's, conflict feels like a threat to your very existence.
- **Lack of Self-Validation:** If you don't validate your own feelings, you'll struggle to assert them in a disagreement.
- **External Locus of Control:** If you believe others control your happiness, you'll avoid upsetting them, even at your own expense.

This fear prevents authentic expression, leads to resentment, and ultimately undermines the trust necessary for healthy relationships.

Principles of Autonomous Conflict Navigation:

1. **Emotional Regulation First (from Chapter 8):** Before engaging in conflict, take a moment to regulate your own emotions. If you're overwhelmed, you won't communicate effectively. Use grounding techniques, take a pause, and breathe.
2. **Focus on the Issue, Not the Person:** The goal is to address a problem or a unmet need, not to attack or blame the other person. Frame your statements around the behavior or situation, not character flaws.
3. **Use "I" Statements:** This is crucial. Instead of "You always make me feel X," use "I feel X when Y happens, and I need Z." This takes responsibility for your feelings and communicates your needs clearly without accusation.
   - *Example:* "You never listen to me!" vs. "I feel unheard when I'm interrupted, and I need to finish my thought."
4. **Clear Boundaries in Conflict:** It's okay to set boundaries during a disagreement.
   - "I need to take a break from this conversation for 15 minutes to collect my thoughts."
   - "I will not tolerate yelling. If we can't speak calmly, I need to step away."

  o "Let's focus on one issue at a time."

5. **Active Listening and Validation (of Others):** While self-validation is key, validating the other person's perspective (even if you disagree with it) can de-escalate tension. "I hear that you're feeling frustrated about X, and I understand why you might see it that way." This doesn't mean you agree, just that you acknowledge their reality.
6. **Seek Understanding, Not Just Agreement:** The aim is not necessarily to "win" or force the other person to agree with you, but to achieve mutual understanding and find a workable solution.
7. **Be Willing to Be Uncomfortable:** Growth happens outside your comfort zone. Navigating conflict authentically is often uncomfortable, but it builds strength and deeper connection.

Practical Steps for Autonomous Conflict:

1. **Choose Your Timing Wisely:** Don't bring up a serious issue when you're exhausted, stressed, or rushing. Find a time when both parties can give their full attention.
2. **State Your Intention:** Start by clarifying your positive intent. "I want to talk about X because it's important for our relationship to feel harmonious."
3. **Describe the Specific Behavior/Situation:** Focus on observable facts, not interpretations. "When you left your clothes on the floor," rather than "You're so messy."
4. **Express Your Feelings (using "I" statements):** "I feel frustrated when..." or "I felt hurt when..."
5. **Explain the Impact:** Briefly explain how the behavior affects you. "...because then I feel like my contributions aren't valued."
6. **State Your Need or Request Clearly:** "What I need is for us to agree on a system for chores," or "Could you please tell me when you'll be late?"
7. **Listen to Their Perspective:** Give them space to respond without interrupting or planning your rebuttal. Ask clarifying questions.
8. **Brainstorm Solutions Together:** Instead of demanding a solution, work collaboratively. "What ideas do you have for how we can address this?"
9. **Agree on a Plan (and Follow Through):** If a solution is found, clarify what each person will do. If not, agree to revisit later.

Chapter 14: Releasing Unhealthy Attachments

As you build emotional independence, an inevitable, and often challenging, part of the journey is recognizing and, if necessary, **releasing unhealthy attachments**. For individuals accustomed to emotional dependence, these attachments can feel like life support, even when they are draining, toxic, or no longer serving your highest good. The fear of being alone, the hope that things will change, or a deep-seated sense of obligation can keep you tethered to dynamics that undermine your autonomy and well-being.

This chapter will guide you through the process of identifying unhealthy attachments and provide strategies for gradually detaching from them, allowing you to reclaim your energy, assert your worth, and create space for healthier connections or a renewed sense of self.

Identifying Unhealthy Attachments: Beyond the Obvious

Unhealthy attachments aren't always dramatic or overtly abusive. They can manifest subtly, often masquerading as "love" or "loyalty." Key indicators include:

- **Chronic Emotional Drain:** You consistently feel exhausted, depleted, or resentful after interacting with this person or engaging in this dynamic.
- **Constant Need for Validation/Approval:** You find yourself constantly seeking their praise, reassurance, or permission to feel good about yourself or your choices.
- **Fear of Disagreement/Conflict:** You avoid expressing your true thoughts or needs because you fear their reaction, anger, or withdrawal.
- **Loss of Self/Identity:** You feel like you've lost touch with who you are, your interests, or your values when you are around this person or within this relationship.
- **Obsessive Thoughts:** You spend excessive amounts of time thinking about the person, their opinions, or how to please them.
- **Difficulty Setting Boundaries:** You consistently fail to uphold your boundaries with this person, feeling guilty or incapable of saying "no."
- **Justifying Unacceptable Behavior:** You rationalize their actions or find excuses for why they treat you poorly.
- **Cycling Between Highs and Lows:** The relationship brings intense emotional swings, where periods of "good" times are followed by dramatic lows, creating an addictive push-pull.
- **Neglect of Other Relationships/Interests:** You prioritize this one attachment above all else, often neglecting friends, family, hobbies, or personal goals.
- **Feeling Trapped or Obligated:** You feel a sense of duty or fear of their reaction prevents you from disengaging.

Why Releasing Is So Hard: The Dependent's Dilemma

Breaking an unhealthy attachment can feel like withdrawing from an addiction because it often taps into primal fears:

- **Fear of the Unknown:** What will happen if I let go? Who will I be without them?
- **Fear of Being Alone:** The very thing emotional dependence tries to prevent.

- **Hope for Change:** The persistent belief that "if only I do/say X, they will change."
- **Guilt and Loyalty:** A sense of obligation or guilt about "abandoning" someone.
- **Social Pressure:** Family or friends might encourage you to stay in a familiar but unhealthy dynamic.
- **Lowered Self-Worth:** If your self-worth is low, you might believe this is "all I deserve" or "I can't do better."

Strategies for Releasing Unhealthy Attachments:

Releasing is a process, not a single event. It requires courage, self-compassion, and a commitment to your own well-being.

1. **Acknowledge and Validate Your Feelings:**
   - It's okay to feel grief, sadness, anger, fear, or confusion when contemplating letting go. Validate these feelings. "It makes sense that I'm scared, as this is familiar."
   - Don't suppress the pain; allow yourself to feel it, process it, and then release it.
2. **Define What's Unhealthy (Objectively):**
   - Journal about the specific behaviors or patterns that are draining you. How do they violate your values or boundaries? What are the tangible costs (from Chapter 3)?
   - Seeing it in black and white can help detach from the emotional pull.
3. **Strengthen Your Inner Anchors (Revisit Part 2):**
   - **Self-Validation:** Remind yourself that your feelings and needs are valid, and you don't need external approval to pursue your well-being.
   - **Self-Responsibility:** Take ownership of your choice to prioritize yourself. This isn't selfish; it's essential.
   - **Boundaries:** This is where the rubber meets the road. Start by setting small, firm boundaries within the attachment. This might mean limiting contact, refusing certain demands, or disengaging from circular arguments.
4. **Gradual Detachment (If Direct Cut-Off Isn't Feasible/Desired):**
   - **Reduce Contact:** Slowly decrease the frequency or duration of interactions.
   - **Limit Information Shared:** Stop oversharing details that can be used to manipulate or drain you.
   - **Disengage from Dramatics:** When the unhealthy patterns arise, consciously choose not to engage in the old dance. "I'm not going to discuss this when you're yelling."
   - **Shift Focus:** Deliberately redirect your energy and thoughts from the unhealthy attachment to your own life, goals, and other healthy relationships.
5. **Build a Support System (Healthy Connections):**
   - Lean on friends, family, or a therapist who support your journey towards independence. These are connections that nurture, rather than drain, and reinforce your decision.
   - This helps to counter the fear of being alone.
6. **Reclaim Your Identity and Energy:**
   - Invest the time and energy previously spent on the unhealthy attachment into nurturing your own self-discovery, hobbies, and personal growth (Chapters 9-11).
   - Reconnect with the parts of yourself you may have lost.

- o *Example:* If you stopped drawing because your partner criticized it, pick up the pencil again.
7. **Seek Professional Support:**
   - o If you find yourself repeatedly stuck in unhealthy patterns, or if the attachment is deeply entrenched (e.g., in cases of abuse or severe codependency), a therapist or counselor can provide invaluable guidance and support.
8. **Practice Forgiveness (of Self and Others):**
   - o Forgive yourself for perhaps staying longer than you should have, or for past actions driven by dependence.
   - o Forgive the other person, not for their actions, but for your own peace. This is about letting go of the emotional grip, not condoning their behavior.

Releasing unhealthy attachments is a brave act of self-love. It's a testament to your growing emotional independence that you are willing to let go of what no longer serves you, even if it's painful in the short term. By doing so, you create immense space for genuine connection, personal flourishing, and a life truly aligned with your deepest values and needs. This freedom is worth every step of the journey.

Part 5: Living an Emotionally Independent Life

Chapter 15: Your Values as Your Compass

Having built the robust foundation of emotional independence – through self-awareness, validation, responsibility, boundaries, and inner strength – you now possess the tools to navigate life with profound autonomy. The final part of this book is about truly **living** that independent life, allowing your inner world to guide your external choices. And nothing is a more reliable guide than your **core values**.

As discussed briefly in Chapter 4, your values are your deepest convictions, the fundamental principles that define who you are and what truly matters to you. For the emotionally independent individual, values are not abstract concepts; they are the unshakeable compass that directs decisions, inspires purpose, and anchors your sense of self, especially when faced with external pressures or uncertainty.

The Power of Value-Aligned Living:

When you live in alignment with your values, you experience:

- **Authenticity:** Your actions reflect your true self, leading to a deeper sense of integrity and congruence.
- **Inner Peace and Contentment:** There's less internal conflict and more harmony when your choices resonate with your core beliefs.
- **Reduced Need for External Validation:** Your compass is internal. You don't need others to tell you if you're doing "right" because you know it aligns with your values.
- **Clearer Decision-Making:** When faced with choices, you can ask, "Does this align with my values?" The answer often becomes clear.
- **Increased Resilience:** Your values provide a powerful "why" that helps you persevere through challenges and setbacks.
- **Sense of Purpose and Meaning:** Living purposefully, guided by what truly matters, creates a deep sense of fulfillment beyond fleeting pleasures.

For the emotionally dependent person, external expectations, a desire for approval, or fear of judgment often override personal values, leading to internal conflict, resentment, and a feeling of being untrue to oneself. Living from your values is the ultimate act of emotional sovereignty.

Revisiting and Deepening Your Values:

Take a moment to reconnect with the values you identified in Chapter 4. Do they still resonate? Have they evolved?

- **Reflect and Refine:** Spend time journaling about these values. What do they look like in action? How do they feel in your body?
- **Prioritize:** If you have many, try to narrow them down to 3-5 core values that are your absolute non-negotiables. These are your guiding stars.

o *Examples:* Freedom, integrity, compassion, creativity, growth, courage, connection, contribution, security, adventure, honesty, justice.

1. **The "Values Check" in Decision-Making:**
   o For any significant decision, pause and consciously ask: "Which of my core values are at play here? Does this choice align with them?"
   o *Example:* If "growth" is a core value, but you're contemplating staying in a comfortable but stagnant job, your values compass will point you toward change.
   o *Example:* If "integrity" is a core value, but you're tempted to gossip, your compass will redirect you.
2. **Values-Based Goal Setting:**
   o Instead of setting goals based on external expectations (e.g., what society says you "should" do), set goals that are directly fueled by your values.
   o *Example:* If "connection" is a value, a goal might be to "Strengthen one meaningful friendship this quarter." If "creativity" is a value, "Spend 2 hours a week on a creative project."
   o This makes your goals intrinsically motivating and deeply satisfying.
3. **Identify and Address Value Conflicts:**
   o Sometimes, your values might seem to conflict (e.g., "security" vs. "adventure").
   o **Action:** Explore these conflicts. Is there a way to integrate them? Can you find a balance? Which value takes precedence in specific situations? This nuanced understanding strengthens your internal guidance system.
   o Also, identify external influences that conflict with your values. Are there relationships, jobs, or environments that consistently force you to betray your core beliefs? This awareness empowers you to make necessary changes (releasing unhealthy attachments, setting stronger boundaries).
4. **Embrace Value-Driven Actions Daily:**
   o How can you embody your values in your everyday interactions and activities?
   o *Example:* If "compassion" is a value, how can you practice more compassion with yourself and others today? If "courage" is a value, where can you show a little more courage?
   o These small, consistent actions build a life of integrity and reinforce your identity.
5. **Use Values for Resilience (Revisit Chapter 11):**
   o When facing adversity, reconnect with your values. They provide strength and meaning. "Why am I doing this? Because I value X, and this challenge is part of that journey."
   o Values can ground you when external circumstances are chaotic.
6. **Review and Reflect Regularly:**
   o Your values might subtly shift or deepen over time. Periodically (e.g., quarterly, annually), revisit your identified values.
   o Ask: "Am I living in alignment with these values? Where are the gaps? What adjustments do I need to make?"
   o This ensures your compass remains accurate and relevant to your evolving self.

Living an emotionally independent life means living a life guided by your deepest truths, not by the shifting sands of external opinion or expectation. Your values are the unwavering anchors of your authentic self, allowing you to move through the world with purpose, integrity, and profound inner peace. This is the ultimate expression of your reclaimed power and the blueprint for a truly fulfilling existence. Dependence that you can stand in your own truth while still valuing the connection you share.

Chapter 16: Purpose, Passion, and Personal Growth

As you continue to build and integrate emotional independence, you'll discover that a natural byproduct is a blossoming of **purpose, passion, and an accelerated commitment to personal growth**. When you are no longer solely defined by external relationships or driven by a need for approval, you free up immense energy and mental space to explore what truly ignites your spirit and drives your unique contribution to the world. This is where living an emotionally independent life truly becomes vibrant and deeply fulfilling.

For the emotionally dependent person, purpose and passion might be externally dictated (e.g., pursuing a career to please parents, adopting a partner's hobbies). Personal growth might be superficial, driven by a desire to be "better" for someone else. For the emotionally independent individual, these pursuits stem from an authentic inner desire and a commitment to becoming the fullest expression of themselves.

The Connection: Independence, Purpose, and Passion:

- **Independence Fuels Purpose:** When you're no longer constantly seeking external validation, you gain the clarity to hear your own inner calling. Your purpose emerges from within, aligned with your values, rather than being imposed from outside.
- **Purpose Ignites Passion:** A clear sense of purpose often unleashes passion – that intense enthusiasm and drive for something you deeply care about. This passion becomes a powerful internal motivator.
- **Passion Drives Growth:** When you're passionate about something, you naturally seek to learn, improve, and push your boundaries. This creates a virtuous cycle of continuous personal growth.

This is the ultimate self-fulfilling prophecy of emotional independence: the more you cultivate your inner world, the more vibrant your outer world becomes, driven by your unique purpose and passions.

Practices for Cultivating Purpose, Passion, and Growth:

1. **Reflect on Your Unique Gifts and Strengths:**
   - What are you naturally good at? What do people ask for your help with? What tasks do you enjoy so much that time seems to disappear?
   - Your purpose often lies at the intersection of what you're good at, what you love, and what the world needs.
   - *Action:* Make a list of your talents, skills, and areas where you genuinely excel or feel a sense of ease.
2. **Explore Your Curiosity and Interests (Unfiltered):**
   - Forget what you "should" be interested in. What genuinely sparks your curiosity? What topics make you want to learn more? What activities bring you joy for their own sake?
   - This is where passion often begins. Allow yourself to explore without needing a "purpose" or outcome.

      o *Action:* Dedicate time each week to exploring something new that genuinely intrigues you, no matter how small or seemingly insignificant.

3. **Identify Problems You Care About:**
   - o What issues in the world (big or small) deeply bother you? What injustices or inefficiencies do you notice? What problems do you feel compelled to solve?
   - o Your purpose might be tied to contributing to a cause or finding solutions.
   - o *Action:* Read widely, engage in discussions, and pay attention to what stirs your emotions – whether it's anger, compassion, or a desire for change.

4. **Connect Purpose to Your Values (Revisit Chapter 15):**
   - o How can your passions and potential purpose align with your core values? This connection deepens your motivation and ensures your path is truly authentic.
   - o *Example:* If "connection" and "growth" are values, your purpose might involve facilitating learning groups for others.

5. **Embrace Lifelong Learning:**
   - o Personal growth is a continuous journey. Cultivate a mindset of curiosity and a commitment to lifelong learning, regardless of age or circumstance.
   - o *Action:* Read non-fiction, take online courses, listen to podcasts, attend workshops, or seek out mentors in areas you wish to grow.

6. **Step Outside Your Comfort Zone Regularly:**
   - o Growth rarely happens within your comfort zone. Purpose and passion often demand that you try new things, face fears, and stretch your capabilities.
   - o *Action:* Commit to one small challenge each month that pushes you slightly outside your usual boundaries – a new skill, a public speaking opportunity, a different social setting.

7. **Practice Reflection and Integration:**
   - o After exploring a new interest or facing a challenge, take time to reflect. What did you learn about yourself? How did you grow? How does this connect to your evolving purpose?
   - o *Action:* Journaling about your experiences, insights, and lessons learned is invaluable for integrating new knowledge and solidifying growth.

8. **Be Patient and Trust the Process:**
   - o Discovering purpose and passion isn't always a linear path. There will be detours, doubts, and periods of uncertainty.
   - o Trust that by consistently showing up for yourself, staying curious, and aligning with your inner compass, your unique path will reveal itself.

Living an emotionally independent life means living a life of active creation, rather than passive reception. It means engaging with the world from a place of genuine excitement and contribution, driven by your unique spirit. As you fully embrace your purpose, immerse yourself in your passions, and commit to continuous personal growth, you not only fulfill your own potential but also become a beacon of inspiration for others. This is the profound richness that true emotional independence unlocks.

Chapter 17: The Ongoing Journey: Sustaining Emotional Independence

Congratulations! You've traversed the landscape of emotional dependence, built formidable pillars of inner strength, and begun to live a life guided by your authentic self. But it's important to remember: **emotional independence is not a destination; it's an ongoing journey**. Life is dynamic, circumstances change, and new challenges will arise. Sustaining your independence means consciously maintaining the practices and mindset you've cultivated, continuously refining your internal compass, and adapting with grace.

This final chapter focuses on how to make emotional independence a lifelong practice, recognizing that "slipping" is part of the human experience, and true strength lies in your ability to continually return to your center.

Why "Ongoing Journey," Not "Arrival":

- **Life's Inevitable Changes:** Relationships shift, careers evolve, losses occur, and new people enter your life. Each change presents a fresh opportunity to test and reinforce your emotional independence.
- **The Lure of Old Habits:** Emotional dependence often has deep roots. Under stress or exhaustion, it's easy to revert to old, familiar patterns of seeking external validation or avoiding discomfort.
- **Continuous Self-Discovery:** You are always growing and evolving. What serves you today might need adjustment tomorrow. Sustaining independence means staying curious about your evolving self.
- **The World Will Always Test You:** External pressures, societal expectations, and the opinions of others will always exist. Your job is to decide how much internal real estate you give them.

Practices for Sustaining Emotional Independence:

1. **Regular Self-Check-Ins (The "Emotional Inventory"):**
   o Make it a consistent practice to pause and assess your emotional state, thoughts, and needs.
   o *Questions to ask yourself daily/weekly:* "How am I truly feeling?", "Am I honoring my boundaries?", "Am I acting in alignment with my values?", "Where might I be seeking external validation unnecessarily?", "What do I need to replenish my energy?"
   o This proactive approach helps you catch potential slips early.
2. **Reinforce Your Foundational Pillars:**
   o Just like a building needs maintenance, your emotional independence pillars need reinforcement.
   o **Self-Awareness:** Continue journaling, identifying triggers, and expanding emotional literacy.
   o **Self-Validation:** Keep practicing compassionate self-talk, especially when facing setbacks.
   o **Self-Responsibility:** Consistently take ownership of your reactions and choices.

- ○ **Boundaries:** Regularly review and adjust your boundaries as your life or relationships evolve. Be prepared to communicate them clearly and consistently.
- ○ **Self-Trust & Confidence:** Keep making and honoring small promises to yourself. Embrace new challenges to build confidence.
- ○ **Embracing Solitude:** Continue to carve out time for self-reflection and inner replenishment.
- ○ **Emotional Regulation:** Practice your coping skills daily, not just when things are tough.

3. **Embrace Imperfection and Practice Self-Compassion:**
   - ○ You *will* have moments where you feel dependent, seek validation, or react from a place of fear. This is part of being human.
   - ○ Instead of self-criticism, respond with self-compassion. "This is a moment of suffering. It's okay. I'm doing my best."
   - ○ Learn from the slip, gently redirect, and recommit to your path. Shame and guilt are counterproductive; self-compassion is your ally.

4. **Cultivate a Strong Support System (Wisely):**
   - ○ Emotional independence doesn't mean isolation. Surround yourself with people who genuinely support your growth, respect your boundaries, and celebrate your autonomy.
   - ○ Be mindful of who you go to for emotional support; choose those who empower you, not those who might unknowingly encourage dependence.
   - ○ Offer support to others from a place of wholeness, not obligation.

5. **Integrate Mindfulness into Daily Life:**
   - ○ Mindfulness helps you stay present and aware of your internal experiences without judgment. This non-reactive presence is a cornerstone of emotional independence.
   - ○ *Action:* Practice short mindfulness meditations, mindful eating, or simply paying attention to your senses during everyday activities.

6. **Celebrate Small Victories:**
   - ○ Acknowledge and celebrate every instance where you assert a boundary, validate yourself, trust your judgment, or choose an independent response.
   - ○ These small victories build momentum and reinforce the positive neural pathways associated with emotional independence.

7. **Seek Recalibration (Professional Support):**
   - ○ If you find yourself consistently struggling, reverting to old patterns, or facing significant life challenges that feel overwhelming, don't hesitate to seek professional support from a therapist or counselor.
   - ○ This is not a sign of failure but a responsible and independent choice to invest in your well-being.

Emotional independence is the greatest gift you can give yourself. It's the freedom to be truly you, to navigate life's complexities with grace, and to engage in relationships from a place of profound wholeness. It is a journey of continuous discovery, resilience, and self-love. Embrace it fully, knowing that every step you take towards your inner strength is a step towards a life of unparalleled authenticity and fulfillment.

Your journey of emotional independence is now truly in your hands. What is one small, tangible step you can commit to taking today to nurture your inner strength?

Conclusion:

The Horizon of True Freedom

You've reached the end of this guide, but more importantly, you've embarked on a profound and lifelong journey. The pages within this book have served as a roadmap, guiding you through the intricate landscapes of **emotional dependence** and empowering you to cultivate the bedrock pillars of **self-awareness, self-validation, self-responsibility, and healthy boundaries**. We've explored how to nurture your **inner strength** through emotional management, self-trust, the embrace of solitude, and unwavering resilience. Finally, we've seen how this inner work transforms your relationships, fostering genuine **interdependence** rather than need-driven entanglement, and how it ignites your **purpose, passion, and personal growth**.

The horizon of **true freedom** is not a distant, unattainable dream; it's the continuous practice of living from your authentic core. It's the quiet confidence that comes from knowing who you are, trusting your own judgment, and navigating life's currents with an **inner compass** that always points you towards your highest good.

Remember, this path isn't about eradicating all vulnerability or becoming an island unto yourself. It's about building a strong, secure inner world so that your connections with others are born of **choice and abundance**, not fear or desperate need. It's about showing up as a whole, complete individual, capable of giving and receiving love, support, and connection from a place of strength.

The world will continue to present its challenges, its temptations for external validation, and its opportunities for growth. Your work now is to consciously apply these principles, day by day, moment by moment. Celebrate your small victories, embrace your imperfections with compassion, and always, always return to the unwavering truth of your own inner being.

You are equipped. You are capable. You are inherently worthy.

Navigating conflict with autonomy means you come to the table as a whole person, ready to communicate your truth and engage respectfully. It transforms conflict from a source of fear and fragmentation into a powerful opportunity for genuine connection, mutual understanding, and ultimately, a more robust and resilient relationship. It's a testament to your emotional in

What is one personal insight you've gained from this journey that you feel ready to put into practice today?

Made in the USA
Columbia, SC
13 July 2025

60522288R00030